BITCOIN CADETS.io

We The People, 4 The People

Together We Are Stronger

Gabriel & Gabriel

WWW.BITCOINCADETS.IO

CONTENTS

INTRO

First, I would like to thank God and you for buying this book, and I hope it will give some sort of inspiration and vision to you, your family, and the people around you. I would also like to thank the bitcoin boy, Andreas Antonopoulos, who has a degree in computer science, data communications, and distributed systems and another one in computer security. He has already published three books and is well respected in the space. He is a profound speaker who discusses bitcoin and the blockchain space.

I would also like to state that I am not a financial advisor. Therefore, you should not take anything I say as financial advice; instead, you should use your own scope and due diligence. I am just a young man who grew up in the city of London, and I would like to share my knowledge of the Bitcoin and the world we live in, also the opportunity that we, the people, have in a new world of programmable money, which has facilitated a financial shift in our economies.

From fiat currency to digital assets, how we, as a People, can link and transact on a global scale using our creative ideas and putting them to practice is reshaping the whole ecosystem, right before our eyes. This entire revolution is about the bitcoin, the blockchain and its decentralized attributes. You see, it's not just about bitcoin, the currency it is about the blueprint and a lot more.

Chapter 1

WHAT IS THE BITCOIN?

The Bitcoin is a peer to peer decentralized, permission less trustless borderless and immutable crypto currency, a value of exchange just like any other real-world currency you may be familiar with. It's different because it is not controlled by any central government, authority or group, and it cannot be manipulated like traditional currencies today. Also, Bitcoin can be transferred in the span of 24 seconds to minutes across the globe with a small transaction fee. This fee can vary from time to time and has resulted in people using faster altcoins to transact if it occurs. What happens in this situation is that the processing of a high number of transactions, all at once in fact makes the blockchain become congested which results in higher transaction fees. This leads to speculations and debates that the bitcoin is not a good medium of exchange, although experts are now calling it digital gold, and a store of value.

After some research I thought that I would take out some of my time to spread what I understand. What we, the people, can do to help the growth of this new piece of technology, it will help the less deprived women and children who are in unfortunate situations. You must remember that the bitcoin is only ten years old and is in its infancy; it runs on its own protocol and is a robust piece of technology.

The functioning of the bitcoin and the blockchain is something that has left many scratching their heads. It has no intermediary for exchange; yes, no third party— you now have your own bank in the palm of your hands. We are currently in the age of digital finance programmable money, at its best in its early days. One does wonder how bitcoins come into play in this age.

Bitcoins are mined by miners who solve mathematical sums using computers with high hashing power, which are then synced together on an algorithm. These huge storage areas of computers use a huge amount of electricity, and the heat from this process often becomes an issue, this in turn causes more large-scale miners to move to lower climate environments, such as

Russia and China. These are places where some of the biggest mining rigs are held.

Today, these large-scale operations are called mining farms. These miners are then rewarded with bitcoins for solving these mathematical equations. You also have small-scale miners who have joined mining pools and are rewarded with bitcoins but on a lower scale. It is said that only 21 million bitcoins will ever be mined in all, and that it will be done by the year 2040.

The mining difficulty increases as a lesser number of bitcoins can be mined every four years. Computer programmers who understand the blockchain language are already in the process of innovating new ideas in the space of our daily lives, and I can say there is some cool stuff out there that would help us in our everyday lives.

I'll give you an example. There's a company that is building a piece of technology using the blockchain technology to check the authenticity of baby food before it is put on supermarket shelfs. We all know that there is corruption in the food industry, and these new innovations that are being implemented is just the tip of the iceberg. You see, what people are forgetting is the fact that it has only been nine or ten years since the bitcoin has taken root. But look how far it has come as a means to society. What I mean is that it has tripled the ratio of gold. Today, as I write this, the bitcoin has not yet become mainstream and has not even captured one percent of the population's attention. Yet with a market cap of over 300 billion dollars, there are not only bitcoins but other crypto currencies that are being born and waiting to be born which are just as good as bitcoins as a medium of exchange and are arguably better.

Chapter 2

What is the Blockchain?

The blockchain is a robust type of hardware which enables a recorded hash pointer as a link from the previous block, to give you an exact transaction data history via the cryptography design. The blockchain is a growing recorded list of blocks all in chain, which is how we get the term blockchain.

A secured blockchain running on a design from a decentralized consensus has also been achieved and makes a good argument for our recording events, such as medical records, land registry, law, and much more. Anything that needs to be accounted for safely can literally be achieved and stored on the blockchain as a ledger of an account that can eradicate fraud.

The invention of the blockchain solves the double spending issue without the need for any third party or authority. The first blockchain was mastered in 2008 and implemented in 2009 by a man named Satoshi

Nakamoto. The blockchain has been a core component in bitcoin and serves as a public ledger for all transactions. Each block contains hash data with a link to its previous block to the next and are all timestamped.

Here is a quick diagram to show how it works.

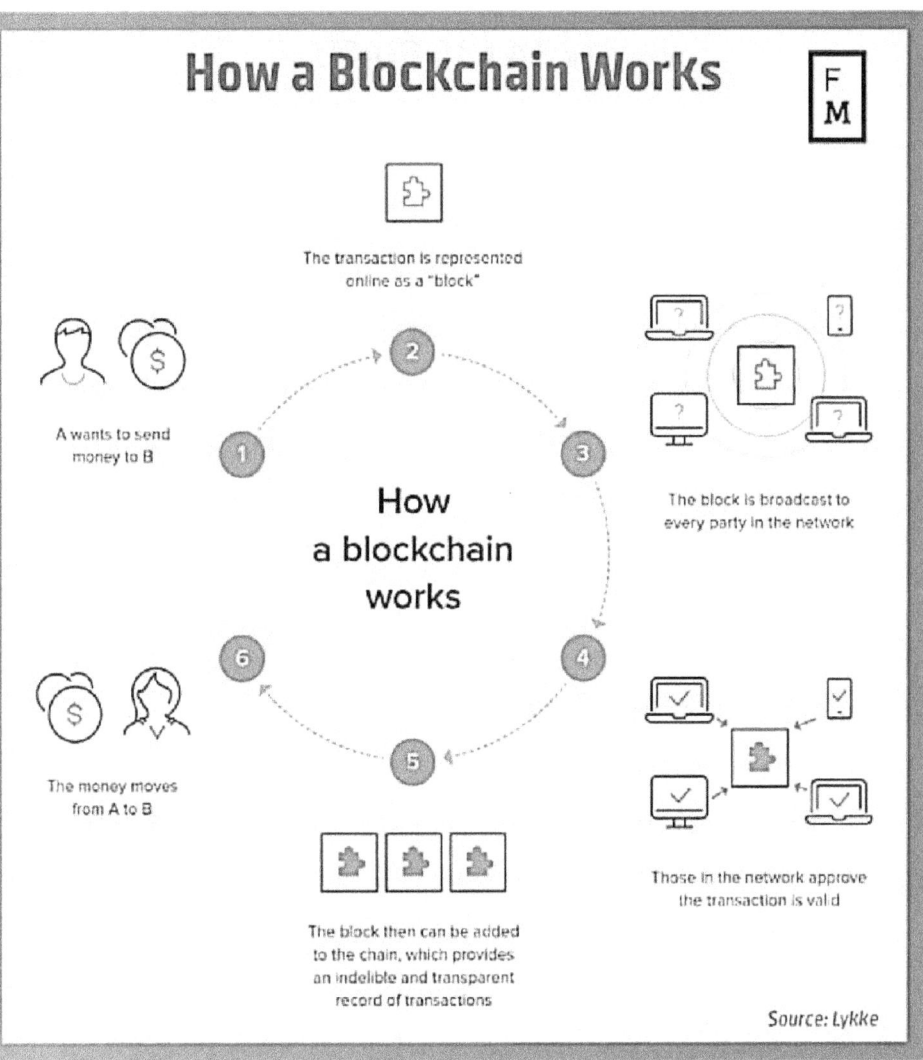

How a Blockchain Works

F
M

The transaction is represented
online as a "block"

A wants to send
money to B

How
a blockchain
works

The block is broadcast to
every party in the network

The money moves
from A to B

Those in the network approve
the transaction is valid

The block then can be added
to the chain, which provides
an indelible and transparent
record of transactions

Source: Lykke

Chapter 3

WHAT IS FIAT?

Fiat is another term for the paper money that we use in our everyday lives. Today, as we look around, we see more online sales than ever before and more digital methods of payments and mobile applications for just about anything. The need for cash is fading out right before our eyes without us realizing it. The blockchain technology being the new powerhouse today, fiat currencies today used to be backed by gold, so if you took your cash to the bank, you would redeem your gold which you initially deposited. This system was abolished by President Nixon in the1970s. The truth of the matter is that the fiat that we use in our daily life's" hold your breath" today is backed by nothing else but the people's confidence that this is a £50 pound note. Fiat is just printed by central banks and fiat currencies inflate—but what does this mean? For we, the people and our children, this means that we lose purchasing power as your currency inflates, which makes the cost of living more expensive therefore, difficulty to provide for our families while our wages stay the same. It has no intrinsic value like gold or silver, and that is the long and the short of it. The bitcoin is not just a currency. It deflates and gains more purchasing power as more people adopt it and make bitcoin a use case. And slowly move away from our traditional banking system which is old and outdated.

Chapter 4

WHAT ARE ALTCOINS?

Altcoins are the alternative to bitcoin cryptocurrency. The word alt means alternative and coins stand for the traditional term currency. These altcoins can also be used as a medium of exchange, and they come under the term digital assets. These assets are available for purchase on the local markets. By buying, holding, selling, or exchanging peer-to-peer, some altcoins hope to overtake bitcoin in its everyday use or as an upgrade to the Bitcoins components.

Chapter 5

WHAT IS THE WHITE PAPER?

The white paper is a blueprint of an asset that intends to come into the crypto space with a potential to bring something new into the digital world. But although some fail, some are identified as scam, I can say for sure that some are here to stay. And this is where investors come in. Some startups make ICOs (initial coin offerings) to the public or to communities with potential investors, who can do their own analysis of an asset through the white paper to see the company's potential and if one thinks it's worth investing in or not. By bringing its use cases to the ecosystem.

Chapter 6

WHAT ARE BITCOIN WALLETS?

There are two types of wallets. Here, we will start with the hot wallet.

Hot wallet;

A hot wallet can be stored on your desktop or mobile device and is a device through which you can send and receive digital currencies through two methods: Using your own unique QR code, which is known as your public key address and what you share when receiving funds. Your private keys, which is used when you are securing one's wallet and funds. However, this should never be exposed to anyone at any given time, or they could gain access to your funds. For sending funds from your wallet, you simply need the public address of your recipient, which you can then use to send funds from your mobile phone or desktop. Storing digital assets on some of these wallets tend not to be the safest, and there have been situations where wallets have been compromised.

Although there are now robust wallets, which are much safer with 12-word backup phases with encrypted technology that only you know, these should always be remembered and kept safe as losing this results in a loss of funds. So, I will again stress this—please keep all your login details and private keys safe and secure. NOT YOUR KEYS NOT YOUR BITCOIN! Famous quote from the great Trace Mayer's profound speaker in the Bitcoin space.

Cold wallets;

Cold wallet storage is off the chain and are not stored on your hardware and is recommended as the safest place When it comes to storing your crypto assets these wallets are known as the Trezor, Ledger Nano s, and a few more. But these are the two that I would recommend storing your Bitcoin on and keeping it secure. Even if you lose your device, if you have your back up phase, you will find that your funds are secure you simply by another device and restore your 12-word backup phase. In most cases, your private keys. Not public but private keys a good idea to remember what term for what your public keys, is always when receiving funds, you can download a Bitcoin wallet on any android or Apple device. Blockchain, Samurai and Zap are all good and reputable mobile and desktop wallets you can start off with. Some wallets also offer the use of debit cards, where one can exchange his crypto into fiat and vice versa This can also be done through ATMs across the globe, where visa is accepted.

Chapter 7

HOW AND WHERE
TO PURCHASE BITCOINS?

The Bitcoin can be purchased online via peer-to-peer bitcoin exchanges, using your debit or credit card you can also purchase Bitcoin by meeting in person and paying in fiat, Or you can purchase it through crypto exchanges, where I am based in, i.e., London, we have several Bitcoin ATM machines available, where you simply put in the amount of cash you would like to spend on bitcoin, then scan your public key address, The bitcoins are then systematically sent to your unique public address that arrives on your phone in minutes. Other options are signing up with an exchange such as Kraken, where you can purchase bitcoin with a debit card. Coinbase is recommended with phone support; however, the recently introduced KYC (Know Your Customer) regulations also apply.

Chapter 8

BITCOIN AND CRYPTO MINING?

Bitcoin mining is what secures the bitcoin network. It scales independently besides bitcoin as a currency. Bitcoins are rewarded as an incentive for helping secure the network. They are only a side effect of mining, On the grand scheme of things. Mining does not only replace central banks but removes security guards, logistics in moving wealth around, gun security, the vaults, buried treasures, safety deposit boxes, security systems, credit checking systems, identity and fraud protection systems you name it You have enormous data centers doing number crunching and running algorithms to find out if fraud is happening. There is five to ten percent loss in the entire payment network every year in terms of fraud and is considered a part of doing business today. There is an argument that mining consumes too much electricity. Well if you look at mining as a payment system then it has in fact, created one of the most efficient secure mechanisms of payment systems in the world today.

Where the electricity argument is concerned, there are many innovations being created for a greener mining concept. Miners will receive bitcoins as reward and incentive for securing the network. Mining farms are usually held in low climate countries such as Iceland, Russia and China, which are reported to have some of the biggest farms to date. The reason behind this is that the heat outflow from these mining farms makes it ideal for them to be held in these types of climate conditions. Mining is also done on lower scales by individuals who join mining pools, but their rewards are much lower purely because of lower hashing power.

Chapter 9

BUYING AND SELLING BITCOIN?

One can buy and sell Bitcoin or crypto assets on an exchange, or peer-to-peer meeting in exchange for cash or via bank transfers depending on the seller's protocol. Another way to do this is to find your local BTM and deposit funds and receive your bitcoins in the space of seconds too minutes at the most or using your debit card, which is accepted by a handful of exchanges. We know that the bitcoin is being adopted more and more as we witness new innovations being built on the blockchain and see more big investors entering this space. With the likes of Richard Branson and Bill Gates jumping on the bandwagon, there have also been reports of a leading crypto currency exchange named Coinbase, which is reported to have had one hundred thousand registrations a day.

Chapter 10

COMMODITIES GOLD & SILVER?

For centuries, gold and silver has always been viewed as a real store of value. I agree but the problem we have in today's society for example I wanted to store or move this asset it comes with heavy precautions.

Imagine trying to move 1 million pounds worth of gold around. Even on a lower scale, it's not tangible enough for our everyday use and as a means of exchange, for example for buying a cup of coffee. Or quick e-commerce.

Since 1971, when President Nixon removed the gold standard and no longer allowed dollars to be redeemed for gold, which resulted in inflation from time to time, but besides this, it gave a huge economic boost to the American dream and economy.

Central banks across the globe have been able to print money at an unprecedented rate. This, in turn, causes debts and leaves us, the taxpayers, to resolve it. As a result, the rich get richer and the poor get poorer and the same old practice continues.

Gold had been used as a currency prior to the gold standard, something that has been spoke about again, but with the new and old digital kids on the block, technology is moving at a tremendous speed. From youth to adults, everyone is waiting to find out what are the latest available apps are for quick daily features.

The new revolution in programmable money is about to take the world by storm. It is said that there are over six billion unbanked people across the globe. This leads to for instance, the exploitation of women, children and food poverty, for starters. However, this list goes on.

Even just having a mobile phone is heaven sent for some people. Being able to actually store and send value through it across the globe in a space of 24 seconds to minutes with small fees without any third party is a game changer.

Being able to become economically involved in peer-to-peer international trade digitally is unbelievable. I think of the times when you need to pay for something but have to wait for third party confirmations to authorize your transaction. The bitcoin and the blockchain can solve matters such as fraud on accounts and other issues, and the greatest thing is that it's the people's currency, so we can all play our part in this digital age.

It is said that there is only 0.5 percent of the population using or involved in crypto currencies today. The other 95 percent are still using fiat and have no knowledge about crypto currencies or even what fiat and its true value is.

Look at the crises in Greece, where hundreds of thousands of people were denied access to their bank accounts, India, where the five-hundred-rupee note was ruled out of circulation by the Government, Venezuela, where the bitcoin was traded for. Ten thousand dollars a coin a few thousand dollars above spot price because of inflation and was a means for people to feed their children, and Zimbabwe, another country with a devalued currency situation, but it looks like it is now bringing the millennial generation to the crypto currency space as their governments continue to show bureaucracy and failed government promises.

The people can now be their own bank and manage it via a mobile phone. If you have travelled to places where the standard of living is low, the cryptocurrency can give huge benefits such as giving people across the globe a chance to live and some sort of freedom. You see, it's not just about bitcoin, the currency. One must look further than this and understand the Bitcoin and blockchain so you and I can spread knowledge to the world and the six billion people across the globe being exploited for one reason or another.

Chapter 11

WHAT ARE ICOs?

ICOs stand for initial coin offerings. These are crowd funded events unregulated as a means by which funds are raised for a new cryptocurrency venture. They take place before a cryptocurrency is born and are sometimes referred to as a utility token or security asset for regulation purposes. Basically, modern day stocks& shares in a digital asset form a percentage of these are sold to public and private investors of the project in exchange for legal tender in most cases. Bitcoin. In the crypto space one can also wait for a token to be listed on the exchange then sell for a higher value. All new tokens have different use cases relating to its project.

Chapter 12

WHAT IS PROOF OF STAKE?

Unlike the proof of work system, in which the user validates transactions and creates new blocks by performing a certain amount of computational work, a proof of stake system requires the user to show ownership of a certain number of cryptocurrency units.

The creator of a new block is chosen in a pseudo-random way, depending on the user's wealth, also defined as 'stake'. In the proof of stake system, blocks are said to be 'forged' or 'minted', not mined. Users who validate transactions and create new blocks in this system are referred to as foragers.

In most proof of stake cases, digital currency units are created at the launch of the currency and their number is fixed. Therefore, rather than using cryptocurrency units as reward, the forgers receive transaction fees as rewards. In a few cases, new currency units can be created by inflating the coin supply, and forgers can be rewarded with new currency units created as rewards, rather than transaction fees.

In order to validate transactions and create blocks, a forger must first put their own coins at 'stake'. Think of this as their holdings being held in an escrow account: if they validate a fraudulent transaction, they lose their holdings, as well as their rights to participate as a forger in the future. Once the forger puts their stake up, they can partake in the forging process, and because they have staked their own money, they are in theory now incentivized to validate the right transaction.

Chapter 13

WHAT IS PROOF OF WORK?

Proof of work is a piece of technology that is difficult and time consuming to produce but easy for others to verify. It satisfies certain requirements the bitcoin uses.

Chapter 14

CENTRALIZED AND DECENTRALIZED APPS VS DAPPS?

Our new and old computer programmers have come up with a very clever consensus for creating these two types of applications: Centralized apps, which are mainly hosted by Google and Amazon servers.

With decentralized apps, your funds are never held by a third party. It is rather held in cold storage on some type of smart contract distributed system where your funds can only be released by a specific code that is unique to you.

So, your funds are more secure than being exposed to hackers stealing funds, although most hackers don't waste their skills on trying to hack thousands of pounds, millions is there go for as it requires a lot of money being spent on in the process.

There is a method through which funds can be sent anomalously so that no one knows where the funds were sourced from. All of this can be done using the blockchains functions.

Chapter 15

WHAT ARE SMART CONTRACTS?

Smart contracts are highly intelligent little programs that execute the transactions between two parties securely. I believe our tech gurus came up with this solution due to the increased situations of hackers stealing funds. As a result, they have now built this robust system of smart contracts.

Chapter 16

MY HISTORY AND FUTURE OF BITCOIN?

Since 2016, I have been watching the crypto currency market cap grow from 89 billion to 1.2 trillion in the space of a year. Though the bitcoin is in its infancy, it now has a market cap of 260 billion I don't think it would be long before bitcoin will overtake the Apple market cap price, thus becoming a leading force in the financial space.

The bitcoin is now reported as the biggest boom in history since the internets.com boom. One may ask whether crypto currencies are here to stay. In my View, they are here to stay. In fact, now we have developers across the globe coming up with new innovations based on the blockchain—decentralized applications where businesses and advertisement companies will be able to cut out all the intermediaries in business and deal directly with the consumer and share some of its profits with the consumer rather than these greedy fat cats.

Individuals will be able to be creative and not have to go through the chores and high fees for selling their own products property owners will be able to rent out their house directly to the tenants all recorded on the blockchain with no estate agent fees. You see you will hear stories of people becoming millionaires or losing money but what we the people need to understand about bitcoin and the blockchain is that this is a new technology that is permission less, decentralized, immutable trustless, borderless and unconfiscatable.

Yes, bitcoin will have its ups and downs, but bitcoin is a deflatable currency, which means that even when fiat currency inflates, the bitcoin will hold its value. In fact, the more it is adopted and used, the more the bitcoins value will increase. Bitcoin is way more than just a currency, and the main source of information that the team at Bitcoincadets.io wanted to let our readers know is that it will help the future of our children and those across the globe who are way less fortunate, through charities that can be set up and run on a totally sincere basis through the blockchain. We also spoke about the exploitation of women and children due to the lack of infrastructure or the many other possible reasons that cause the six billion people to be without food or shelter. So, we encourage the people to see bitcoin not only as just a currency but also grasp a deeper understanding of the technology. We know for sure that Bitcoin is about to reshape not just our financial system but a whole new way of life of logistics and finance a digital payment system for almost anything all done with cryptocurrencies. Remember, bitcoin does not inflate like our traditional fiat currencies.

Which causes such problems in our world today We want the people to understand that only 0.5 of the population are involved in crypto currencies today, but what a brilliant job it has done to date. Is phenomenal Bitcoin is not even mainstream yet, although there are certain merchants who are accepting it as a medium of exchange, Japan and Sweden being amongst the first regulators to accept crypto payments as a means. In these countries you can buy property and cars using bitcoin. So, it is slowly getting there. We, the people, are slowly becoming curious about the bitcoin's ability, the apps and dapps that can be built upon it, what it provides to the people and how we all can transact on the scale of visa and beyond. With a high volume of transactions per second, even small low-income families can now earn passive incomes from blockchains running on their own algorithms. There is so much going on in this space, and we, at Bitcoin Cadets.io, are on the verge of opening a charity fund for the less deprived across the globe by making them aware of the financial shift also helping them gain access to these financial applications and let them know there is another gate of open source finance. We feel bitcoin is about its protocol giving less unfortunate educated people freedom to financial markets. People are able to transact without the involvement of a third party. One may ask what about crime, but we say that the same crime is committed today with cash and its traditional system. One must have his or her own privacy as a means to get by and be able to transact no matter what race or religion or lack of intelligence, one should be able to be free in these areas. And we see bitcoin as the answer to this. We ask the people to be mindful about your securities and keep an open mind and advise anyone to learn about the bitcoin and the blockchain and what is being created in the new world of digital assets We need everyone to understand that we, the people, are together stronger. Thank you, I digress, we hope you enjoyed the read and was of some benefit, inspiration, and determination for the future of the women and youth across the globe for whom cash has failed for one reason or another. May god bless you. Thank you for reading me.

Gabriel & Gabriel

WE THE PEOPLE 4 THE PEOPLE

WWW.BITCOINCADETS.IO

List of recommended crypto exchanges for purchasing bitcoins:

BINANCE.COM

KRAKEN.COM

KUCOIN.COM

HUOBI.US

List of recommended wallets:

Blockchain info wallet; mobile and desktop

ZAP wallet; mobile and desktop

Wirex mobile and desktop

ECLAIR; wallet; mobile and desktop

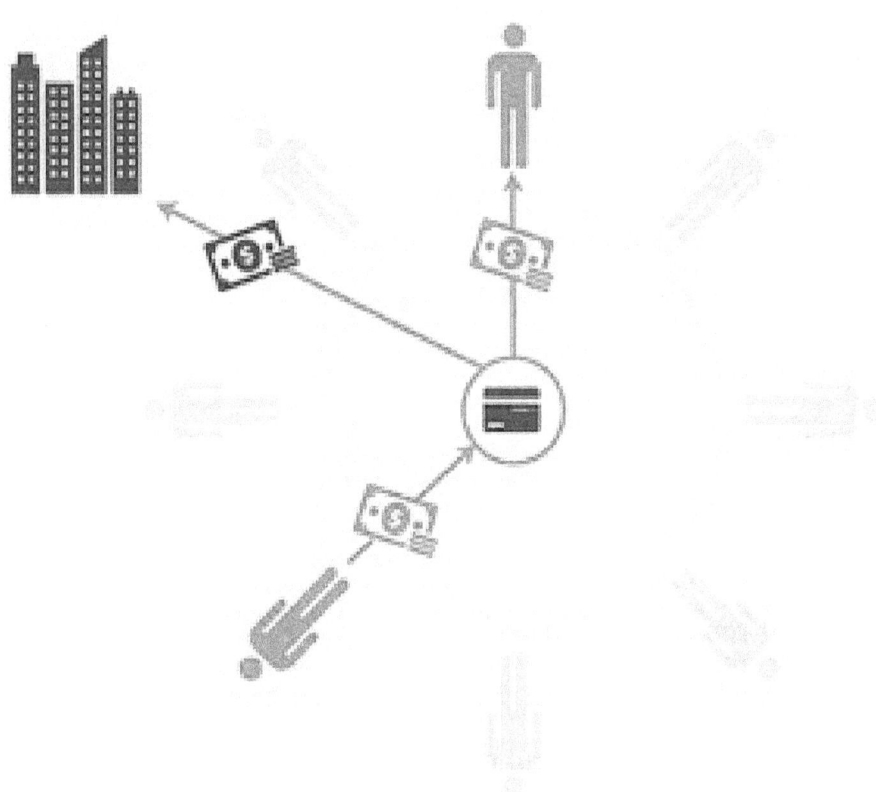

Current payment systems require third-party
intermediaries that often charge high processing fees …

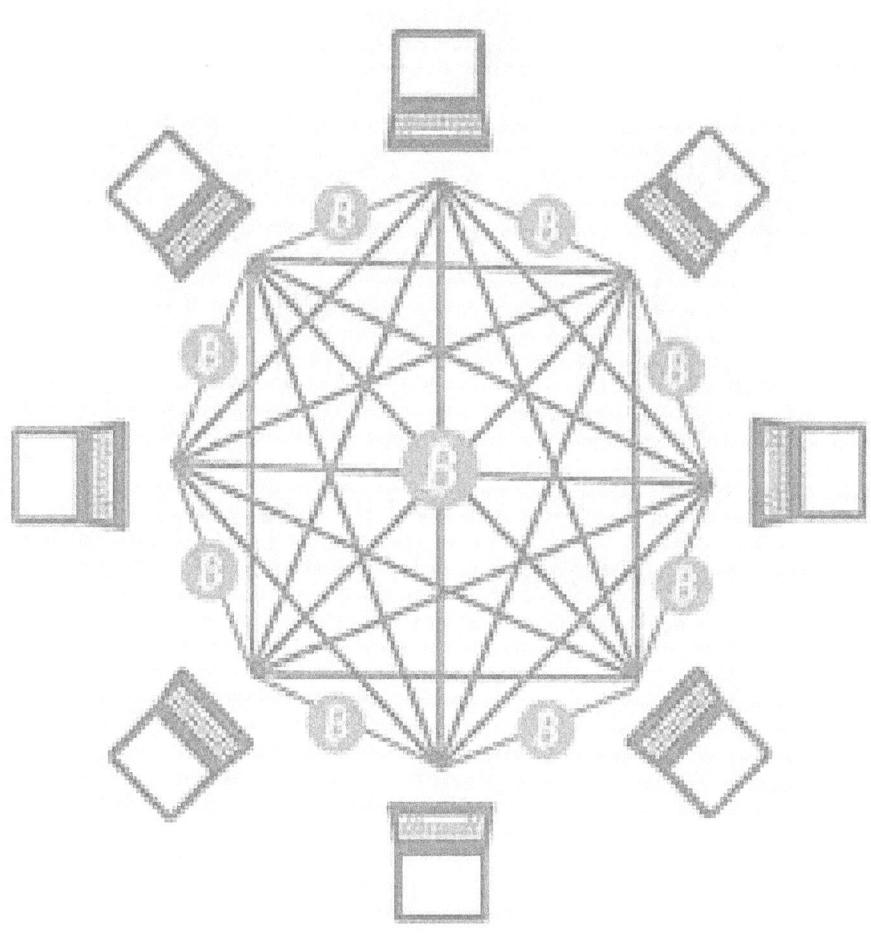

… but machine-to-machine payment using the Bitcoin protocols could allow for direct payment between individuals, as well as support micropayments.

SATOSHI CONVERTER

1 Satoshi	= 0.00000001 BTC
10 Satoshi	= 0.00000010 BTC
100 Satoshi	= 0.00000100 BTC
1,000 Satoshi	= 0.00001000 BTC
10,000 Satoshi	= 0.00010000 BTC
100,000 Satoshi	= 0.00100000 BTC
1 million Satoshi	= 0.01000000 BTC
10 m Satoshi	= 0.10000000 BTC
100m Satoshi	= 1.00000000 BTC